D1275461

The Flock
on the Dock

Kelly Doudna

Consulting Editor, Diane Craig, M.A./Reading Specialist

ABDO
Publishing Company

Published by ABDO Publishing Company, 4940 Viking Drive, Edina, Minnesota 55435.

Printed in the United States.

Credits
Edited by: Pam Price
Curriculum Coordinator: Nancy Tuminelly
Cover and Interior Design and Production: Mighty Media
Photo Credits: AbleStock, Brand X Pictures, John Foxx

Library of Congress Cataloging-in-Publication Data

Doudna, Kelly, 1963-
    The flock on the dock / Kelly Doudna.
       p. cm. -- (First rhymes)
    ISBN 1-59679-481-X (hardcover)
    ISBN 1-59679-482-8 (paperback)
       1. English language--Rhyme--Juvenile literature. I. Title. II. Series.
PE1517.D627 2005
808.1--dc22
                                                                    2005048028

SandCastle™ books are created by a professional team of educators, reading specialists, and content developers around five essential components that include phonemic awareness, phonics, vocabulary, text comprehension, and fluency. All books are written, reviewed, and leveled for guided reading and early intervention reading, and designed for use in shared, guided, and independent reading and writing activities to support a balanced approach to literacy instruction.

Let Us Know

After reading the book, SandCastle would like you to tell us your stories about reading. What is your favorite page? Was there something hard that you needed help with? Share the ups and downs of learning to read. We want to hear from you! To get posted on the ABDO Publishing Company Web site, send us e-mail at:

sandcastle@abdopub.com

SandCastle Level: Beginning

-ock

block

clock

dock

flock

rock

This is a .

Look at the .

Here is a .

See the .

Here is a .

The block is in a city.

The clock is round.

The dock is flat.

The flock can fly.

This rock is hard.

The Flock
on the Dock

There is a big flock.

The big flock
sits on the dock.

18

The big flock
sits on the dock
until six o'clock.

Each day at six o'clock, the flock from the dock flies around the block.

Each day at six o'clock, the flock from the dock flies around the block to rest on a rock.

About SandCastle™

A professional team of educators, reading specialists, and content developers created the SandCastle™ series to support young readers as they develop reading skills and strategies and increase their general knowledge. The SandCastle™ series has four levels that correspond to early literacy development in young children. The levels are provided to help teachers and parents select the appropriate books for young readers.

Emerging Readers
(no flags)

Beginning Readers
(1 flag)

Transitional Readers
(2 flags)

Fluent Readers
(3 flags)

These levels are meant only as a guide. All levels are subject to change.

To see a complete list of SandCastle™ books and other nonfiction titles from ABDO Publishing Company, visit www.abdopub.com or contact us at:

4940 Viking Drive, Edina, Minnesota 55435 • 1-800-800-1312 • fax: 1-952-831-1632